# This World of Wonder

*A SELECTION FROM BOOKS BY HAL BORLAND*

*High, Wide and Lonesome*
*Country Editor's Boy*
*The Dog Who Came to Stay*
*Penny*
*The Youngest Shepherd*
*King of Squaw Mountain*
*The Amulet*
*When the Legends Die*

# This World of Wonder

by Hal Borland

Illustrated by Peter Zallinger

J. B. LIPPINCOTT COMPANY
Philadelphia and New York

The following chapters were first published as articles in *Humpty Dumpty's Magazine*: The Seed, The Grasses, Insects and Wings, Shooting Stars, Migrant Birds, Leaf Colors, Snow, The Sun, The Ice Ages, The Awakening.


Printed in the United States of America
First Edition

U.S. Library of Congress Cataloging in Publication Data
Borland, Hal Glen, birth date
This world of wonder.
SUMMARY: Describes nature's annual cycle month by month—colored leaves, ice and snow, hibernation, and sprouting seeds.
1. Natural history—Juvenile literature. [1. Natural history. 2. Months] I. Zallinger, Peter, illus. II. Title.
QH48.B783 500.9 72-12827
ISBN-0-397-31453-1 

# Contents

FOR BARBARA

*With whom I listen to the birds,*
*name the wild flowers,*
*and count the stars.*

# *April*

## THE SEED

April is a time of wonder, when the spring peepers emerge from hibernation and begin to call, when robins and redwing blackbirds come back north, and when new green life appears. That is one of the greatest of all wonders, the growth of a bud and a leaf from a seed or a root that has lain dormant in the earth all winter.

Hold a seed in your hand, a round, brown radish seed, and there is no sign of life in it. It gives no hint that something inside its smooth, hard skin can become a leaf, a stalk, a blossom, a root. In fact, a radish seed looks like a tiny pebble, which is utterly lifeless. But put that seed in the ground, give it water and warmth at a proper time, and something inside begins to quicken. The tides of spring days and spring sunshine urge something inside to burst that hard little shell and send down a root and send up a leaf to open in the air and reach for the sunlight. That seed will sprout and begin to grow.

What happens, of course, is that there is a germ of life inside that radish seed, just as there is a germ of life in every seed and in every egg. Nobody is quite sure where life came from, but we do know what it does. It grows, and it creates more seeds that will grow, in their own time, so that life goes on and on. Some of that life is the green life we call plants, and some of it is the red-blooded life we call animals. Some of that life is rooted in the soil, and we call it trees and grass, and radishes. Some of it is free to move from place to place, and we call that kind of life birds and insects and animals and people.

A radish seed can lie in the ground all winter, waiting to sprout, until the daylight is long enough and the sunlight is strong enough for the plant to grow. When it does sprout it will always be a radish, not something else even though the seed itself may look like a mustard seed or a turnip seed. Something inside that hard little shell has the pattern for its growth as well as the germ of its life, just as something inside an acorn has the pattern for an oak tree.

There is yet more within a seed that adds to the wonder. It has a sense of time and weather which makes the clocks, calendars, thermometers, and wind gauges that

we use to measure things seem crude by contrast. By long study and difficult calculations, humans have learned the rhythms and sequences of the sun and the moon, the tides and the seasons. We have built our calendars and almanacs around these calculations. But a seed or a root, without eyes or what we call a brain, without making any calculations at all, seems to know all about the sun and the seasons, the weather and the climate.

How does a seed know when to sprout? How does the sap at the roots of a maple tree know when is the proper time to start to move up toward the waiting twig and leaf and bud? What is it that tells a tulip bulb to send up leaves to catch the sunlight and begin to shape a flower bud? What mysterious force prompts one seed to wait in its sprouting till all danger of frost is past, while another seed sprouts at that precise moment when its stem and leaf can survive ten degrees of frost but not twelve or fifteen?

We have answers, of a sort, in terms of temperature and length of daylight. But those really are reports of how the seed or bulb or root responds, not why. None of our knowledge explains the hidden force within the seed or root. We have elaborate apparatus to measure the sun's warmth and the soil's moisture and even the pressure of sap in a tree. But how does a radish seed measure such critical conditions?

Somehow, these conditions are measured by all living things that spread green leaves to catch sunlight and make food for themselves. They know when April comes, and they respond. And that is the great, enduring wonder of springtime.

# May

## THE GRASSES

When we think of spring and the green world, we usually think first of grass, of the lawn or the park or the hayfields and pastureland in the country. Grass grows almost everywhere except in the deepest woodland and the driest desert. It flourishes wherever there is soil and moisture and a few weeks of summer warmth.

We are more dependent on grass than on any other species of plant life. We could live without trees, though we would miss the shade and have to find something other than wood for fuel and lumber. We could do without the beautiful flowering plants, though we would miss the color, the fragrance, and the beauty of them. But without grass we would starve. We would have neither bread nor meat. All cereal grains are grasses—corn, wheat, rye, barley, oats, rice. All our meat animals, those that provide beef and pork and mutton, eat grass in some form. Grass also anchors the earth's soil against erosion and helps check floods. Grass cools the earth and the air and is constantly renewing the oxygen in the air we breathe.

Grass is among the humblest of all visible forms of plant life, even though its seven thousand species do include such giant plants as bamboo. Few ordinary grasses grow more than three feet high, and most of the grasses that clothe our plains and flatlands are much shorter than that. Yet grass is so insistent and so efficient in sprouting and growing that it outnumbers all other plants. Perhaps someone has counted the number of individual grass plants on an ordinary suburban front lawn, but I have never found the figure. It must run well into the millions.

Grass spreads in a multitude of ways. Some grasses have stems, either on the ground or underground, which send up new shoots at every joint. But most spread by seed. Grass has flowers so small and so simplified that we seldom notice them. Those flowers have no petals, because they do not need insects to fertilize them. They have stamens which release pollen finer than dust. This pollen is carried from flower to flower by the wind, and when pollen reaches the pistil in a flower it fertilizes the ovary. That is what creates the seed. When the seed

ripens we sometimes notice it because the seed head on a grass plant turns golden tan and sheds the seed.

The seeds of many grasses are so small that they, like the pollen, can be carried by the wind. Often grass seeds have tiny, buoyant hairs that catch the air currents, like thistledown, and ride them surprising distances. Investigators, gathering insects and other forms of life from airplanes, have trapped grass seed almost a mile above the earth.

Some grasses have spines on their seeds that attach themselves to passing animals and ride to new areas. Sheep, with their thick wool, constantly carry grass and weed seed into new territory. Cattle, horses, and such wild animals as rabbits and foxes do the same thing. And man has unintentionally carried grass seeds all over the world. Several African and Caribbean grasses came to North America two hundred years ago in ships carrying hay to feed cargoes of livestock. All the old trade and caravan routes were lined with strange, exotic grasses carried there by men and their animals.

Nearly all plants are able to renew themselves after being cut or broken off, but grass is outstanding in this ability. Break off or cut one stem and another stem soon grows to take its place. Mow a hayfield and within a week there will be new growth from the shorn grass plants. Our suburban lawns have to be cut at least once a week, they renew themselves so fast all summer.

Grass is such a minor form of plant life and has so little "skeleton" that only minor evidence of it is ever found among fossils in rocks. We know next to nothing about its origin and only a little about its history. Long before Man existed, during the Miocene epoch perhaps 50 million years ago, when the Great Plains of North America were being slowly lifted out of the seas, the common reed, one of the grasses, apparently was growing in the marshlands all across this continent. And one of the cord grasses, a marsh grass still common in salt marshes, spread its roots and stems, trapped silt, and changed vast marshlands of the Midwest into the deep, black soil that still covers much of the area from the Allegheny Mountains to the High Plains. The grasses were here long ago, helping to build soil and hold it against the wash of rain and the rasp of wind. And except for those grasses that make up so much of our farm crops, grass is very little changed from what it was when man first looked around him and saw that the world was green and friendly for him and his own kind.

# *June*

## WEEDS

Dandelions open their fat yellow blossoms along the roadside, in vacant lots, and on grassy lawns. Some people think they are beautiful, but most people call them weeds.

Daisies come to bloom in rural pastures and along back streets in the towns and cities. People who love wild flowers pick them and put them in vases, but farmers say they are weeds and wish they could be rid of them in their fields.

Soon the milkweeds that grow in low meadows and beside rural brooks are in blossom, with sweet, heavy fragrance. The big black and orange butterflies called Monarchs feed on milkweed leaves, and the white juice from milkweed stems was used in medicine at one time.

But most people call the plant a weed, and even the name says it is—milkweed, the weed with a milky juice.

What is a weed? Why do most people call the beautiful dandelions and daisies weeds? Why was the fragrant, useful milkweed called a weed to begin with?

The simplest answer is that any plant that grows where it is not wanted is a weed.

Most of those plants we call weeds insist on growing where we want other plants to grow. The farmer wants grass and clover to grow in his meadows and pastures, and he doesn't want daisies there. People with lawns that they want to keep green and neatly clipped want nothing but grass to grow there, so dandelions are weeds to them. And as for milkweed—well, it grows in pastures and hayfields and even in flower gardens and vegetable gardens if it isn't watched, because its seeds are carried long distances by the wind. So milkweed is a weed to most people.

Strangely, many of the weeds we have today were cultivated plants to begin with. Many of them were garden flowers. Others were used by herb doctors to heal sick people. And some were used for food. Dandelion leaves were eaten as cooked greens or raw in salads, and they still are by some people who like natural foods. Daisies were garden flowers. So was that wild pink we call bouncing Bet whose roots were once used for soap, especially for washing women's hair. Chicory, the tall wild

plant with the beautiful blue flowers, is still grown in Europe for its roots which are dried and ground with coffee beans to make a special kind of coffee.

Nearly all the clovers that grow in America, both wild and tame, came from Europe originally. So did the bright yellow buttercups that are so common in early summer in every rural pasture. And wild carrot, with that big white head of bloom known as Queen Anne's lace, was brought from Europe as a garden flower. Milkweed, however, was a native flower here in America and spread its sweet fragrance, followed by its shimmering puffs of floss-borne seeds, long before Columbus sailed across the ocean.

Some of these plants were brought here by early settlers to grow in their gardens. In time their seeds blew or were carried into the surrounding fields and grew there. They became what are called "escapes" and they naturalized themselves. They liked this soil and this climate and proved they didn't need gardens in which to grow. Some other plants were brought here by accident, some in straw and litter in ships that carried horses or cattle, some in seeds that were brought here to plant, mixed in with wheat or oats, perhaps. Once the seeds arrived here and had soil to grow in, they took root. If they were hardy they made more seeds and spread.

Other plants came when their seeds hitchhiked from

someplace far away. Some seeds have hooks or spines that catch in the fur of a passing dog or rabbit. Some are stick-tights that cling to a trouser leg or a stocking until they are plucked off, perhaps days later and miles away. Some seeds, like dandelions and milkweed, have fluff that acts like a parachute and the wind can carry them for miles. Birds carry seeds in mud on their feet and hard seeds pass through their stomachs unharmed. Many seeds, of trees particularly, float down rivers, across lakes, out to sea, and take root in distant places. And human travelers have spread seeds with their trash and their leavings wherever they have gone. New plants always grew up along the old caravan routes. Later they grew along the railroad lines. Today you find them along the big highways and around the major airports.

So there are wild flowers, and there are weeds, depending on what people want. There are those beautiful dandelions on the lawn, and to most people they are weeds. But if you pick a bouquet of them they are flowers. And if you take one of their hollow stems and blow on it just right, so that it makes a musical note or two despite the bitter taste of the juice, it is even a musical pipe of the kind that country folk played a long time ago.

A weed isn't a weed unless you think it is.

# July

## INSECTS AND WINGS

Only four kinds of creatures ever learned to fly on their own wings: the insects, the now extinct flying lizards, the bats, and the birds. The insects were the first to take wing, before any of the others even existed. Maybe the power of flight enabled the insects to persist through thousands of centuries, for it made them able to escape earthbound enemies. Fossil insects almost 200 million years old have been found, and among the most ancient insect fossils are wings with no traces of the bodies that bore them.

Insects seem to have changed little over the eons. Many fossil insects are almost identical with those we know today, particularly cockroaches, dragonflies, certain beetles, ants, and bees. Some of those ancients no doubt would be completely at home in our woods and fields today. There is every probability that ants and bees, at least, have been the same kind of creatures they are as far back as we can trace them. And it seems certain that they were what we call social insects, which live in communities and share the work.

Those who have studied such matters say only twenty-four separate families of insects ever evolved "insect societies." Those we know today include only the bees, the ants, the termites, and some beetles.

A society calls for teamwork, for some enduring instinct, and ability to act as a group toward a common purpose. A swarm of flies or mosquitoes definitely is not a society; it is an unorganized group in which each individual is working for itself. A hive of bees or a hill of ants is a community, with assigned tasks for every member of the colony and an organized system of work and living.

There is a rigid caste system in almost every ant colony. Most of the members are infertile females, which cannot lay eggs and reproduce. They do the work of the colony, from gathering food and building complex nests and tunnels to caring for the eggs, the pupae, and the larvae that eventually grow into adult ants. The males are drones and do no work. They are tolerated in the colony only because eventually one of them will mate with a new queen. Sometimes the males are also the colony's soldiers, the fighters, but not always. The ant queen is the heart of the colony, petted, fed, and kept prisoner inside the nest. She lays all the eggs.

Periodically new queens are hatched. At a proper time these queens and the males grow wings and are released from the colony. They take flight and the queens are mated in the air. The queens return to the earth, bite off their wings, and find sites for new nests. The males die soon after the nuptial flight. Each solitary queen digs a tunnel into the ground where she has chosen the site for her nest, and when she has an underground room to suit her she begins to lay eggs. She tends the eggs until the first ants of her new colony are born. They are infertile females, workers. They go to work at once, knowing by instinct what to do, and enlarge the nest. They care for the queen, who never again emerges into the open, and she lays more eggs, which the workers tend and feed as they become pupae and larvae. A new colony has been started.

Scientists seem to agree that most ants have some capacity for pleasure and anger. They have keen senses, with eyes that apparently cannot detect color as we can but can see ultraviolet rays, which are invisible to us. They have "touch hairs" on the body that are sensitive to vibrations and through which they probably hear

sounds. They are sensitive to heat and cold. There is no evidence that they feel pain. An ant with its whole abdominal section cut off will continue to eat honey with apparent pleasure. One researcher finds that 95 percent of an ant's actions are instinctive, 4 percent are the result of habit, and that only 1 percent can possibly be the result of anything like intelligence.

Perhaps that is one reason the ants have been here so long. They do everything necessary for the welfare of the community without having to think about it. Each ant has a certain place and certain work to do and it cannot expect ever to be or do anything else. Only those born to be queens can be queens. And only young queens and males who may mate with them ever grow wings. They are the only ones who can fly away from the colony, and the males die soon after their flight. Perhaps long, long ago all ants had wings. Then they found safety in tunnels underground and didn't need wings, so the workers stopped growing them. But somehow the thrill of flight persisted as a part of the ritual of mating. Or perhaps flight is the best way to distribute the young queens and scatter the new nests. Even in the plant world that happens, for the mikweed, the thistle, and many others send their seed out on wings to start new colonies.

# *August*

## *SHOOTING STARS*

Most clear, dark nights you can see a shooting star, as we call it, if you keep looking. Those shooting stars are meteors. They are points of light that suddenly appear in the sky, like distant stars, race across the darkness, usually toward the horizon, and disappear.

For a long time nobody knew what a meteor was. But finally those who study stars and the sky decided that a meteor is a piece of a comet that exploded long ago. Those pieces are still wandering about the universe in huge, looping paths that follow the original comet's orbit. There are uncounted pieces of such comets out there in the depths of space. Periodically clusters of them come close to the earth's orbit, or path around the sun. Most meteors are small, probably only a few inches in diameter, but when they enter the earth's atmosphere the friction makes them white-hot. Then they look big as stars streaking across the darkness.

There are half a dozen meteor showers each year. Each is named after the constellation from which it appears to come. The biggest of all, the Perseids, named for the constellation of Perseus, occurs on the 10th, 11th, and 12th of August. The next largest, the Leonids, named for the constellation of Leo, comes on the nights of November 14, 15, and 16. Another, the Andromedids, which is not quite so big, comes from November 17 through 23. There are other meteor showers in December, January, April, May, and July, but none of them is as big as those in August and November.

Most people watching meteors will be satisfied if they see ten or twenty in an hour of watching. On special occasions, however, the meteors seem to come in droves. The most remarkable meteor shower I ever heard of was seen by a distinguished astronomer, Professor Denison Olmstead, of New Haven, Connecticut, on the night of November 12, 1833. He was watching the Leonids, which seem to come from directly overhead and race downward toward the horizon in all directions. He reported that meteors fell "like flakes of snow." He estimated that he saw 240,000 meteors in nine hours that night. He said they ranged in size from mere streaks of light to "globes of the moon's diameter." If he had not been a notable astronomer whose accuracy was beyond question, such statements would seem ridiculous. But there is no reason to doubt what he reported. He had seen one of the most unusual meteor showers ever reported. What he watched should be called a meteor storm rather than a shower.

I once watched the August Perseids with an astronomer on a hilltop in open country, and in two hours we counted almost a thousand meteors. That was the most I ever saw at one time. And we were bitten by one mosquito for every meteor we saw. After that I tried watching for meteors in November, when there were no mosquitoes. But the most I ever saw in November was about one hundred meteors in two hours of watching.

The amazing thing about these meteor showers is that they come year after year. Professor Olmstead saw all those Leonids in November of 1833, but if you watch for meteors this year you almost certainly will see them on the same nights he saw them. They will come next year, the year after that, and for countless years more. Your grandfather saw them, and your grandchildren will see them if they look for them.

Occasionally a meteor reaches the earth. Then it is called a meteorite and it is valued as a sample of the vast mystery of the deep space in the sky. Scientists examine it, try to guess what it was to begin with, where it came

from, what it is like out there. Nobody ever learned very much from the meteorites except that they often contain a great deal of nickel and iron.

Only a few large meteorites have struck the earth. The largest we know about fell in Arizona many centuries ago and made what is now called Meteor Crater, a hole about a mile across and 600 feet deep. Some Indian legends of the Southwest tell of a big fire that fell from the sky and ate a huge hole in the earth, so this big meteorite may have fallen since man first arrived in America, perhaps twenty-five thousand years ago.

Other big meteorites have fallen, in ancient times, in Texas, in Argentina, in northern Siberia, in South-West Africa, and in Greenland. A meteorite weighing more than thirty-six tons was found in Greenland and now can be seen in the Hayden Planetarium in New York City. Millions of meteors have flashed across the night sky, but only a few large meteorites have ever reached the earth. Never in all the centuries of written history has there been a report of anyone being struck by a meteorite.

# *September*

## *MIGRANT BIRDS*

Every autumn many birds travel from north to south for the winter. They migrate from the North to escape the cold and to find a place where wild seeds and insects on which they feed will not be covered with snow or frozen in the ground. Next spring they will go north again and build their nests and raise their young.

There are various patterns of migration. Some birds that spent the summer in the South migrate to South America. Some that nested in the far North move only a few hundred miles south. Others travel tremendous distances. The Arctic tern, which nests in northern Alaska, farther north than any other bird, flies as much as 10,000 miles in migration to spend the winter on the shores of Antarctica.

But when we talk of migration we usually think of the songbirds going from northern United States down to the southern states. Most of those songsters migrate, as do a great many other species. We don't know what tells them when to go or what route to follow. All we know is that the birds know when and how to go. The swallows leave early, and so do the warblers. Most of them are gone from the North by September. Then the woodpeckers we call flickers gather in flocks, but they usually wait till October to leave the North. Not all robins migrate, but those that do usually leave the North before the end of October. Orioles leave early, but brown thrashers often wait till hard frost before they go.

Probably it is shortening daylight that tells the birds when to start south. All birds are sensitive to light and darkness. They have a kind of clock and calendar in their bones that keeps track of the seasons and the daylight. Wild geese seem also to have a special weather sense. Sometimes Canada geese don't leave the North till late November, then take off ahead of the first snowstorm.

Nobody has yet learned how birds know where to go when they migrate or how to get there. Some think they have built-in compasses, or a sense of direction that responds to the earth's magnetic currents as a sailor's compass does. Others think they can measure the sun's angle, as a navigator does, and know where they are. Shore birds are believed to have a special sense of direction.

Even more mysterious than how they know where to go is the way young birds know how to get there. In some species the young birds, those hatched only last spring, travel in different flocks and at different times from the older birds. Yet these young birds that have never gone south follow the same routes and go to the same places the older birds do. They never get lost or go to the wrong place.

Smaller birds, such as warblers, bluebirds, finches, and some thrushes, sometimes travel in mixed flocks. I have seen as many as five species in the same flock. They travel mostly in daylight and stop early in the afternoon to feed and rest. Robins usually travel by themselves but in big groups, a hundred or more in one flock. Flickers also travel by themselves but in flocks of only twenty or twenty-five. Hawks are sometimes seen migrating in large numbers, hundreds, in loosely organized flocks.

Most small birds are rather leisurely in their travel. They go south only a little faster than autumn itself, which progresses only about sixteen miles a day. This means that if the first hard frost comes to northern Connecticut on September 25, it will reach southern New Jersey and Maryland the first week in October, about ten days later.

The small birds usually fly quite close to the ground in

migration, seldom more than a few hundred feet in the air. Geese and hawks, however, usually fly high. Canada geese commonly fly a mile or more above the earth. And the big birds often fly long distances between stops. One flock of geese is known to have flown nonstop from James Bay, Canada, to Louisiana, about 1,700 miles, in sixty hours.

On occasion small birds also fly surprising distances without stopping. Ruby-throated hummingbirds, the only hummingbirds in the northeastern states, migrate overland to Florida or Louisiana, then all the way across the Gulf of Mexico to spend the winter in Central America. That span across the Gulf is 500 or 600 miles. It seems impossible that a bird weighing less than half an ounce, about the same as a first-class letter in the mail, could fly that far without stopping to eat, drink, or rest. But those hummingbirds have been doing it a long, long time. That is another of the big mysteries about bird migration.

# October
## LEAF COLORS

Autumn is color time in the woodlands. It happens in many places over the world, but the most brilliant display of colors comes in North America, and the most spectacular of all is along the eastern part of the continent. This is because there is a greater variety of trees and because autumn there usually is dry and sunny, with mild days and chilly nights. There are also special autumn colors in the Great Smoky mountains of the Carolinas, in the Missouri Ozarks, and in the mountains of the West, where the aspens seem to be streams of gold pouring down the mountainsides and the scrub oak is red as rubies, all with a background of pines and spruces.

It used to be thought that frost made the color in the leaves. An imaginary elf named Jack Frost was supposed to go around with a pot and brush and paint all those leaves. Now we know that is all wrong. Frost doesn't color the leaves. If hard frost comes too early it withers and blackens the leaves before they have any color. The Jack Frost story hasn't any truth in it.

The coloring of the leaves is a part of the natural change that comes when summer ends and the trees begin to prepare for winter. All summer long those leaves have been making food for the trees. That is their purpose. In a way even our best chemists cannot explain, the chlorophyll, the green coloring matter in the leaves, takes moisture and carbon dioxide from the air and with sunlight as energy it makes sugar and starch and oxygen from them. The sugar and starch feed the trees. The oxygen is released into the air and helps keep it clean enough for us to breathe. That is one reason trees are so important—they make oxygen for us to breathe.

When summer nears its end the trees begin closing up shop for the winter. They are better off without leaves in the winter. So they begin withdrawing their sap to the roots and cutting off the leaves. Little layers of cork form at the base of each leaf to plug the sap veins. With no more sap bringing fresh chlorophyll to them, the leaves begin to fade. The old chlorophyll dies and loses its green color. Then yellow and orange pigments that were in the leaf all summer can be seen. These pigments are carotene, the same substance that makes carrots yellow and orange.

Then the sun begins to change sugars and acids that were left in the leaves when they were sealed off. They produce reds and purples. And finally a brown substance

called tannin, which is common in oaks and was long used to tan leather, appears in the leaves, especially in the oaks. Tannin may be combined with the yellow carotene or with the red pigments, which are called anthocyanins, to make the tan and russet and burgundy and purple leaves that are often seen on the oaks.

In most woodlands the first leaves to turn are those of the shrubs and bushes, the lower plants. Perhaps this is because they must end their season early. Quite often little sapling trees will also color early. In the edge of the woods you may find a maple seedling not two feet high with all its twelve or fifteen leaves a bright red while the big trees around are still green. But huckleberries and wild blackberries and all the viburnums also color early. After them come the most vivid reds of the soft maples, usually in the valleys. The dogwoods begin to turn deep red then, too. Then the sugar maples turn red and orange and yellow, and the ash trees turn almost blue and purple. And the sassafras and the gum trees turn all shades of red and yellow and orange. Then, just when the maples begin to fade, the oaks take over, the early ones sometimes with bright tans and yellows, the later ones with deep reds and purples and chocolate browns.

Sometimes a tree, usually a big maple, will hold all its yellow or orange leaves until a morning after a hard frost. Then, though there isn't a whisper of a breeze, the leaves will begin to fall, first a few, then more, then a real storm of leaves. I have seen the big sugar maples in front of our house do this and stand knee-deep in sunny yellow leaves by midmorning. What happens is that mist in the night air crept into those corky layers at the base of the leaves. The frost turned it to ice, which pried the leaves loose but held them in place as long as it was frozen. When the sun rose and began to warm the air it melted that ice and released the leaves. Those on the outside, in full sun, fell first, but as the sun reached farther into the tree it loosened more and more leaves until they came down in that gleaming snowstorm of yellow.

Usually the leaves come down a few at a time. That little cork is not too easily loosened. But a light rain or even a heavy dew makes the leaves heavy enough to break free. And a gusty wind can take a whole cloud of colorful leaves from every tree it touches. Finally all the leaves come down and cover the floor of the woodland, protecting the tender plants and the roots from winter cold and eventually turning to leaf mold and feeding the soil for all the trees.

# November

## THE ANCIENTS

When the leaves have fallen from most of the trees except the evergreens, sunlight can reach the floor of the woodland and we then can see some of the oldest plants there are on earth. They are called club mosses, though they are not mosses at all in the sense we usually mean. They look like tiny cedar trees and pine trees that grow in groves less than a foot tall. Because they grow from stems that trail along the ground under the leaves they are sometimes also called running pine.

More than 300 million years ago, in what geologists call the Paleozoic era, these little plants were trees bigger than most of our pines today. Great forests of these trees, with gigantic tree ferns and other long-vanished species, grew in the marshy lowlands. Earthquakes buried these forests and eventually they were turned into the underground beds of coal we mine today. Ordinary coal was formed from the trunks and limbs of the trees. Special fine-grained cannel coal and the black mineral we call jet were formed from the vast deposits of spores from the club moss trees. The spores, which were fine as dust, were the plants' means of reproducing before plant life evolved seeds. Ferns and mushrooms still reproduce by spores. It seems impossible that those ancient trees could have produced enough spores to make veins of coal several feet thick, but they did.

Over the millions of years many changes occurred in trees. The pines and firs and hemlocks that we know today came into being, and trees like maples and willows and birches, which drop their leaves each autumn, took form. But all the while those club moss trees persisted, although they shrank in size. First they became small trees, then they became bushes, and finally they were reduced to creepers, the form we know today. But they never changed their way of reproduction. They kept producing spores, great quantities of those dust-fine spores. They are so small and so uniform in size that at one time they were used for microscopic measurements. They are so soft and soothing to the tongue that they were used on pills that are hard to swallow. They were used as we use talcum powder, to soothe chafed skin. And because they burn quickly and with a bright flame they were used for years in fireworks and for flashlight powder in photography.

The plants themselves have long been used in making holiday decorations, particularly Christmas wreaths. Every year yards and yards of these evergreen creepers are gathered in the woods and sold along with Christmas trees and other holiday greenery.

There are two principal kinds of these club mosses. One is often called ground cedar, and its shoots look like tiny cedar trees. Its branches even have overlapping scalelike leaves, and its creeper stem, which reaches along the ground beneath the cover of dead leaves, sending down roots here and there and sending up a shoot like a miniature tree every foot or so, has those scalelike leaves. Its color is a bright, lively green.

The other form is often called running pine or ground pine, and its shoots have the appearance of a pine tree's sprig. Its leaves are needlelike, something like those of a fir tree since they grow all around the stem, not on one side. One member of this species, called staghorn club moss, has branches like a small tree and sends up special shoots with spore heads that produce the best club moss spores, called lycopodium powder.

They have their own place in the sun from now until next April, when new leaves begin to appear on the trees

beneath which they grow. They are evergreen and will be just as bright when the snow covers the ground as they are in November. They are the real ancient ones. Their kind saw the land when the giant lizards ruled the world. They saw the first birds take wing and were here when the first bird song made an echo. They were here when the big ice sheets plowed down from the North. They were here when the first men came, when they learned to light a fire to warm themselves and to protect their caves from the saber-toothed tiger. They were here when man tamed the dog and the horse.

They are still here. I find them every time I go up the mountainside into my own woodland. In the summer I sometimes have to hunt for them because they are hidden in the deep green shade. But in late autumn I never fail to see them. This is their season in the sun. When I bring a few strands of them down to decorate our doorway for the holidays I will be bringing something from the very ancient past to remind me how old is this earth and how young is man.

# *December*

## SNOW

Snow is beautiful. This is sometimes hard to believe if you live in a city where snow turns to slush in the streets and seldom has a chance to swirl into drifts as graceful as a bird's wing. But even there it makes beautiful patterns in the air as it falls. In the country, of course, it lies where it falls and makes white magic of a meadow and a wonderland of the woods. And snow falls almost every year somewhere in all the states of the United States except Hawaii.

Snow, of course, consists of snowflakes, and the snowflake is one of the most beautiful, delicate crystals in the world. Put on a dark coat or take a square of dark cloth and go out into a snowstorm. Catch a few flakes on your sleeve or the square of cloth, and stay out where it is cold and look at them. Unless they are broken or clotted together, each flake is some variation of a six-pointed star. The points usually are elaborate as lace, and each point on a flake is exactly like the other five. But no two flakes are alike.

This seems impossible, but it is one of the marvelous things about snowflakes. People who have studied and photographed them have looked at thousands and thousands of those six-pointed flakes but they never have found two exactly alike. There aren't enough numbers to count the flakes in one snowstorm, but those who know say that even in that unbelievable number there are no two alike.

Each of those beautiful, intricate flakes is so fragile that the gentlest touch of a finger can break it and one warm breath can melt it into a tiny droplet of water. Go back into the warm house and every snowflake on your sleeve will be gone in less than a minute. All that will be left will be a few tiny damp spots. Yet those fragile flakes make drifts that can block a highway. In the mountains they pile up and become so heavy they turn to ice and form glaciers that gouge rocks out of the mountainside as they move slowly toward the valleys.

A snowstorm, even a quiet one, soon begins to shape its own pictures and to change the world. Watching the flakes fall you can see how the wind moves, how it eddies

and curls around trees and bushes. The snow makes it possible even to see the wind itself. On a road or driveway you can see how the wind, with snow in it, flows almost like water. When it comes to a tree beside the road it curls around the tree, then curls back before it goes on, and the snow begins to pile up where the wind curled back. It makes a drift. It even makes a little drift behind the brown stem of a dead goldenrod.

That is the way the wind makes sculptures of itself, in snowdrifts, which can be as graceful as the flight of a swallow in summer. As the snow keeps on falling it puts white caps with high crowns on the thistles in the pasture and at the roadside. If the wind stops, the snow puts high dunce caps on the fence posts. If it is a wet snow it outlines the limbs of the trees and makes the branches black as ink. It puts white capes on the pine trees and the hemlocks, and when the wind strikes them the trees shrug off those capes in rushing snowslides that make little snowstorms of their own.

As the snow covers the countryside the world becomes a brand-new place. The meadow is a big, fresh page on which the rabbits and the foxes and the field mice will write adventure stories tonight. The brook flows between fresh banks that have curls and swirls and scallops along their tops and no scars or gashes anywhere. The rocks on the hillside are huge cupcakes mounded with white icing, or tremendous pebbles of gleaming white marble, whichever you wish to see. The old apple trees have big white nests in their high crotches where robins raised their fledglings last summer. In the bushes beside the old stone wall the nest where sparrows raised a brood last summer has been roofed over for winter quarters and now is a miniature igloo with field mice instead of Eskimos living in it.

For a little while, after the snowstorm, this is a whole new world. Those snowflakes that melted at one warm breath have come in so many uncountable billions that they have changed everything in sight. Eventually it will be a world of snowplows and snow shovels, of sleds and skis, of boots and mittens and mufflers, and of slush and ice and mud. But now it has been made a special place that nobody ever saw before, simply by the creation of those fragile flakes of snow in a mass of clouds overhead.

# *January*

## THE SUN

Winter days are short, we say, meaning there are fewer hours when we can see the sun than there were last summer. The nights are longer, so the total length of the days, from one noon to the next, is the same. But last July we could see the sun fifteen hours or more each day, and now in January we can see it only a little more than nine hours. And the sun seems far off to the south instead of being overhead, even at noon. This is because of the way the earth's axis is slanted and the way it turns on that axis. That is also the reason January is winter in North America and summer in South America and all the other places south of the equator.

One of the strange things about all this is that the earth really is closer to the sun in January than it is in

July. Now the sun is only 91,400,000 miles away. Next summer it will be 2 million miles farther away. This is because the earth's orbit, the path it follows around the sun, is shaped like an egg instead of a ball. If it were a perfect circle we would always be the same distance from the sun.

The sun is the center of what we call the solar system. The earth and eight other planets travel in orbits around it. The sun is a very hot star and is believed to be a huge mass of gases that burn with intense heat and provide the heat and light that make it possible for people and animals and plants to live on the earth.

As nearly as our astronomers can measure it, the sun is more than one hundred times the diameter of the earth. It is so big that if the earth were put inside it there would be room enough for the moon to continue in its present orbit, more than 225,000 miles from the earth, and still be inside the sun. If you can imagine the earth as small as a grain of sand, the sun would be bigger than a baseball.

The sun's temperature has been measured at 6,000 degrees Centigrade. This is more than twice as hot as the carbon arc, one of the hottest flames we use to melt metal. It is this heat, filtered through the air and clouds so that it does not burn us to a cinder, that creates all the energy there is on earth. It evaporates water from oceans and lakes, the vapor forms clouds, then it falls as rain or

snow. The rain cools and waters the earth and makes it possible for plants to grow. Using the energy of the sun in their green leaves, plants make sugars and starches and grow roots, stems, more leaves, and fruit or seeds. Thus the trees grow, and grass and corn and wheat and potatoes and oranges. Animals and people are kept warm by the sunlight and they eat food created by plants with the help of sunlight. The meat we eat comes from animals that ate plants. So all the energy we have to move about and to work and think and talk comes from the sun one way or another.

The energy we use to heat our houses, to make light, to drive our machines, and to make our automobiles run all comes from the sun. Some of it is electricity made in power plants at the big dams, where falling water turns the generators. Some is electricity made in steam plants that burn oil or coal, and some is from atomic plants. The coal and oil and gas were formed from green plants and animals that ate plants many millions of years ago. They were buried by earthquakes and squeezed by the weight of rocks deep in the earth until they changed into coal or petroleum. The uranium used in the nuclear reactors of atomic power plants got its intense power from the sun many millions of years ago in ways we do not yet understand.

All the things we use in our daily lives owe a debt to the sun. The lumber in our houses and in our furniture comes from trees that could not grow without sunlight and rain. The cotton and linen for cloth comes from plants nourished by the sun, and the wool is from sheep, the silk from silkworms, both of which eat plants. The fibers of nylon and rayon and all the other man-made fabrics are made from things that grew in the sun, needed it to grow. We would not have metal for our machines and our tools if we did not have the fire with which to smelt the metal from the ore. Everything we use to make that fire owes its energy to the sun.

Without the combination of sunlight, air, and water the earth would be as lifeless and dismal as the moon. Sunlight by itself is not enough, as we know from studying the moon, which has sunlight but neither air nor water. Without air and clouds to shield it, the moon is intensely hot in the daytime and intensely cold at night. It has no oceans, no lakes, no streams, and no water to nourish plant life. Without plants or water, it has no oxygen for animal life to breathe.

We have water and we have air, and we have sunlight, too. With all three we have a great variety of plant and animal life. And we can survive even in winter, because we have sunlight.

# February

## THE ICE AGES

Every winter we have snow and ice, but even the worst winter we will ever see cannot begin to compare with the long, long winters the earth knew long ago during the Ice Ages.

Nobody knows what caused them, but several times in the remote past large parts of the earth were covered with tremendous glaciers, sheets of ice that came down from the North and changed the whole surface of the land. In places the ice was more than a mile thick. It covered mountains. It filled valleys. It lasted for thousands of years. Some think the ice came and stayed because of a shift in the ocean currents. Some think eruption of volcanoes filled the air with smoke and ash so that the heat from the sun was cut off. Some think the earth shifted on its axis so that climates changed in many places. But nobody really knows.

The last great Ice Age occurred since North America had its present shape, with its mountains and major valleys. It began about one and a half million years ago, and there were great changes in climate for the next million years or more. Four times, at least, the ice sheet advanced southward and retreated. At their greatest southward point, the glaciers covered almost one-third of the land on the globe. The last of those great sheets of ice did not melt back and free the northern half of North America until ten or fifteen thousand years ago.

These great sheets of ice locked up so much water that all the oceans were much shallower than they are today. Probably the oceans dropped between 150 and 300 feet. This uncovered a huge bridge of land between Alaska and Siberia, where the ocean is quite shallow even today. Over that land bridge came the people from Asia who were the ancestors of the American Indians. For some reason, pehaps because that land bridge dammed back the cold water from the Arctic Ocean, most of Alaska and western Canada were not covered by the ice. So those ancestors of the Indians came across the land bridge and down the Pacific coast and spread out across America.

Meanwhile the ice was doing strange things to the land. It was plowing its way southward and scraping

rocks and soil from every hill and mountain in its path. We can still see the deep scratches on some mountain rocks where the ice used harder rocks to carve its path. With its huge load of sand and rocks and soil, which it pushed along like a bulldozer, the ice dammed up all the rivers it touched. Then as it melted back, bit by bit, it released floods of water that made new channels and became new rivers. And it gouged out great hollows in the land where it could plow away the soil and get down to bedrock. Those hollows became lakes. The Great Lakes of today were formed by the ice.

Some of the big, shallow lakes the ice formed were filled with sand and soil as the ice melted back, and these became vast meadows or plains—areas of flat land in the East, not the High Plains of the West, which were largely untouched by the glaciers. Upper New York State is one of those areas flattened by the ice, and the Finger Lakes are what is left of all the water from ice that melted there.

Besides shaping the land, the glaciers changed both the plants and the animals and even the birds of the land it covered. As it came south it stripped off the trees, of course, knocking them down like straws. And it covered all the grass and leaves that deer and bison and elk and moose eat, so they were driven out. Without those animals to eat, the big cats and wolves and bears left, too. And without seeds and insects for food, most of the birds went away.

But the effect of the ice did not reach far ahead of it. The constant melting at the southern edge created heavy fogs and somewhat eased the cold. Not far ahead of the ice there must have been a rather mild, very damp climate. And each time the ice melted back a little farther, the birds and animals and the trees and plants crept northward again. The seeds were carried by the wind and by birds and animals, just as they are today.

Ice formed many of the hills we have today, with the sand and gravel it dropped as it melted. Long Island was formed of such material pushed along by the ice and dropped when the Ice Age began to end. The rugged coastline of all New England was formed by the ice, too. Its melting first gouged out deep rivers across the land to the ocean. There were a great many such streams to carry off all that water. Then the ocean rose, as the ice melted, and it slowly came into the mouths of all those new rivers. When the ice had melted back into Canada, the flow in most of those rivers stopped and they were simply valleys. But at the shoreline they were coves and inlets and harbors. They still are, only because long, long ago the Ice Ages brought winters that lasted thousands of years.

# March
## THE AWAKENING

Spring is an awakening of buds and bulbs and of all the animals that hibernate, or sleep, through the winter. In the North, this time is marked by the calling of the spring peepers, tiny tree frogs whose scientific name is *Hyla crucifer*. That simply means a hyla or tree frog, with a mark shaped like an X or a cross on its back. They begin to trill soon after they emerge from hibernation. That is their mating call, and some think it sounds like the tinkling of sleigh bells. Some say it is only a shrill "Peep, peep, peep." But it is one of the clearest signs of spring.

Even when fully grown, these little frogs are only about an inch long. They are very hard to find for they are the color of dead leaves, they live in damp lowlands, and they trill loudest at night. They are true frogs and they lay their eggs in the water. The eggs hatch into tadpoles, lose their tails, and become adult tree frogs. Sometimes they trill again on warm autumn evenings, but not nearly so many of them nor so loudly. When it begins to chill off toward winter they dig into the mud of a swamp or a shallow pond and sleep till spring.

Most cold-blooded creatures that live in the North hibernate. That is because this is the only way they can live through the cold weather. Their blood always is near the temperature of the air around them and would freeze in their veins if they stayed out in the open. In the South, where winters are warmer, they either do not hibernate or they go to sleep later and wake up earlier. Frogs, toads, snakes, turtles, salamanders, and some fish hibernate.

Warm-blooded creatures, such as dogs and cats and deer and rabbits and people, do not have to hibernate. Their bodies "burn" some of the food they eat and keep their blood warm the year round. Some scientists have suggested that the big lizards, such as the dinosaurs which ruled the earth 200 million years ago, died off and disappeared because they were cold-blooded and the climate changed. It became cold and the Ice Ages started. And because many of those lizards were bigger than an elephant they could not burrow in the mud as a frog or a turtle does and hide from the cold. So they died.

Of all our warm-blooded animals, only bats and woodchucks hibernate every year. Bats hide in caves where they hang by their toes and sleep for weeks, living on fat stored in their bodies. We seldom see them, even in summer when they are fully awake, because they are active only at night.

But the woodchuck spends most of the summer in the fields and meadows and can be seen almost any day. It really is a big cousin of the squirrel that happens to live in a hole in the ground. In late summer it lays on a thick layer of fat, often increasing its weight by one-third. Then when days turn chilly it goes into its den, closes the entryway behind it, curls up, and goes into a deep sleep. Its body temperature drops from 96.8 degrees to as low as 38 degrees. Its pulse drops to one beat every several minutes. Instead of breathing five or six times a minute, it breathes once every five minutes. It doesn't waken to eat or drink. It stays in that deep sleep till about the time the spring peepers peep. Then it rouses, unplugs its den, comes back into the open air, and looks for food and a mate.

In a way, that is what the peepers do, too. They have to wait till the outside air is around 50 degrees, however, for several days in a row. Otherwise their blood doesn't flow properly and they can't move about or catch food or "sing." If a cold wave comes after they emerge from hibernation, they go back into the mud till it passes.

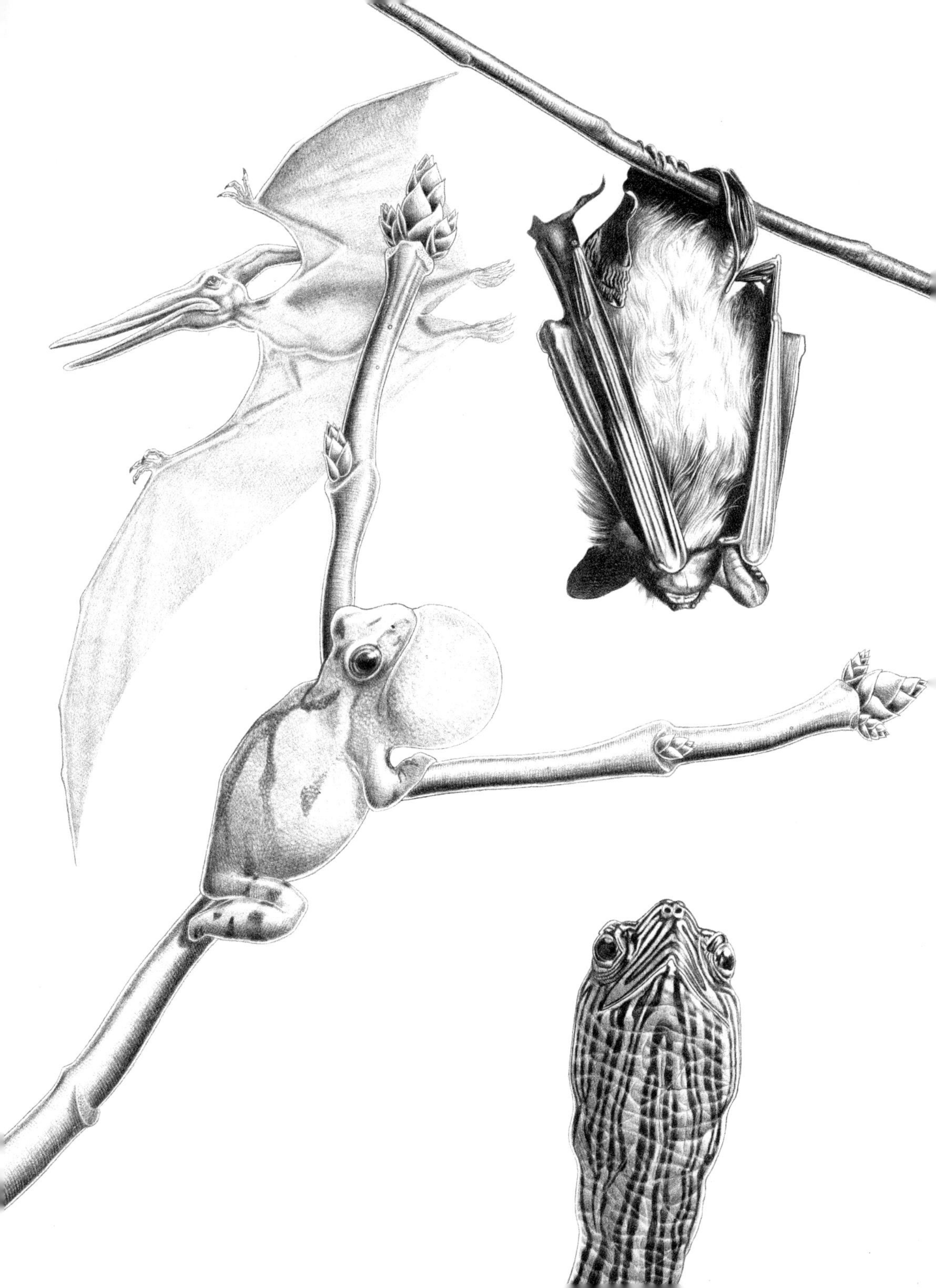

It once was thought that bears hibernate. Now it is known that they do not. They simply sleep a great deal. But their body temperature drops only a few degrees, and they can be awakened. When they are wakened from a winter nap they are often in a bad temper. Chipmunks may hibernate in some very cold parts of the North. Usually, though, they merely sleep somewhat as bears do and waken from time to time and eat from the stores of seeds and nuts with which they stock their dens each autumn. Squirrels sometimes stay in their nests and sleep several days during a winter storm. Skunks and raccoons also do this. But squirrels and skunks and raccoons never really hibernate. They are out foraging for food through the winter months, even with deep snow on the ground.

All the winter sleepers, however, both those that hibernate and those that merely sleep more than usual, waken when the spring peepers announce that spring is here. By then they have had their rest, most of them are hungry, and they are ready to start their busy spring and summer lives.